Jan

CW00920016

adversaries/
comrades

Best wishes
Gail Aldwin

by Gail Aldwin

with a foreword by Ian Stephen

First published in the UK in 2019 by Wordsmith_HQ (formerly The Student Wordsmith)

ISBN 978-0-9928241-6-7
Printed and bound in the UK.

Wordsmith_HQ
www.wordsmithhhq.co.uk
Loughborough, UK

Cover illustrations by Emily Suzanne Young.

For Izzy and Jonny

Foreword

It was a busy week at the Scottish Creative Writing Centre, Moniack Mhor, set in the rising slopes of open moorland. These open outlooks somehow helped tutors and students to look inwards. Our subject was fiction, but when Gail Aldwin asked if I'd take a look at some of her poems, I thought, *why not? It's all language.* Once I opened the file and began to read, I knew at once that this was a writer who took to the craft of verse in a serious and a playful way, at the same time. The poems seemed to be considered but still lively. That thought is now confirmed by the pleasure of reading this first pamphlet.

Exploration of form is obvious in the range from prose poems to pattern poems. The focus on theme gives some of these something of a hint of George Herbert though there is often a wry or wistful, even quirky, slant which is more akin to Emily Dickinson or even E.E. Cummings. Yet, the influences are absorbed in a natural way, so already there is a voice coming through that is identifiable as Gail's alone. The imagery is as clear and bold as gripping a steering wheel as though it were a lifebuoy. The selected word is sharp as only a whetted edge can make it and yet it never seems fancy. This can give the effect of something close to the sinister, in a true fairy-tale way that is more disturbing than lulling. Take this one line:

'His hair is straight as pins and his eyes are a shade of pea.'

Most writers, in any genre, take a while to build up their skills and maybe a bit longer to learn that the holding back is part of that skill set. For me, Gail has an intuitive grasp of that already. More, she has a very clear eye and the poems come over as emotive but honest. The sentiment is expressed but wit is permitted:

'You can't do maths on my half-sister because she's whole to me.'

It takes confidence to allow that long line its natural stretch. This is a strong and moving pamphlet and I consider myself fortunate to have had the chance to enter into it in advance of its publication.

Ian Stephen
January 2019

Ian's most recent book, *Waypoints* (Bloomsbury),
combines memoir with poetry and stories retold.

Contents

Birthday

In a bubble of memory,
he smells of talc and breast milk.
Heavy in my arms, he rests under my chin.
I tilt my head to keep him cocooned.

How to survive

Turn the paper lengthwise and fold into a rectangle.
Boulders tumble and pebbles scour,
Flip the bottom right hand corner and level the sides.
watch the plumes above the swell,
Drop the left hand corner down and line up the edges.
silky seams spreading salt and tears.
Turn the paper over to let the long ends meet.
A lip of quiet contains the bulging mass,
Tuck the triangles into the pockets created.
a rush turns strands to curls of spume.
Stretch out the base to make a boat and place.

Ginger, Ginger

Heartbeats clobbering, faces tight with anticipation, three of us four are scrunched behind a wall. Still now, we listen, our faces angled to hear a rapping yet silence hovers. Bobbing heads, we check he's there. With twitching fingers he grasps the handle, reaches tip-toe, to **knock-knock.** His footsteps pelt, we duck and huddle. Our scapegoat scrambles to the nest, the littlest of us all. Minutes pass, our breath becomes a symphony of sighs. The Carpenter's front door groans as Old-Girl steps out, her curls scooped into a hairnet, pom-poms on her slippers: *who's there?* From side-to-side she turns, screws-up her eyes, scowls at the empty street. We glimpse her out of sorts, keep fingers at our mouths to supress sniggers. My oldest brother can't resist, pops his head above the bricks, *boo,* he shouts. She hears, goes inside but leaves the door hanging open like a dislocated limb. Slumping back to the trench, we are lined up like sticks, rigid with delight and fear. We think she's got a gun or an axe or she's vanished up her baggy knickers. Giggles start, we can't hold them, they spew like foam. *Boo who?* she calls, broom in hand, she makes her way. No flying over rooftops for Old-Girl Carpenter. Instead, she thrashes the handle over heads and legs. We scatter, dazed and stumbling. Our scapegoat springs tears and cries: *boo-hoo.* Old-Girl Carpenter brushes fag ends into the gutter. **Who's the joke on now?**

Fractions

Amelie isn't cracked down the middle
she can't be split into equal parts
or shared out like a chocolate bar.
You can't do maths on my half-sister because she's whole to me.

Family menu

Dad says my little sister's good enough to eat.
Her skin is the colour of runny honey:
spread her on toast.

My little sister's mum's called Agnes.
She's tall and thin like a cinnamon stick:
stew her with apples.

Me and my brother look the same:
strong and sleek as a swan's wing.
We're meat for a banquet.

Girls' Brigade

Loot crimps stems of waxy flowers around a wire frame.
She wedges the crown, uses kirby grips to secure and I
walk, balancing the honour bestowed. Other girls
hiss, saying it's not right. She has her favourites:
long-haired blonde girls always get to be May
Queens. Doesn't matter that my sister took
the role two years before, it's the fair ones
who score the prize. They don't know
money has changed hands, glasses
at The Legion clinked, a deal
secured. Dad suggests we
call her Auntie Loot
but the name
doesn't
stick.

She goes

Our Mum doesn't like to say the same thing twice.
It's not okay to keep repeating herself.
But when will we ever learn?
Dear Lord, how many times?
If she has to say it again she'll go mad.
But it's not our fault: we've heard it all before.

Fastenings

Unlace the strings that strap me tight
a corset of contempt.

Pick hooks from eyes so I can see
contours to overcome.

Snap the popper fastenings loose
find freedom from constraints.
The Velcro spots are next to go
break down the pity and spite.
Don't speak to me of duty,
don't tell me what to do.
Threaded is my needle
ready for the work.

Sew up your lips
to seal you in:
a button for
your mouth.

Weep

Mum can't believe I pushed her –
it's shameful to do such a thing.

But it was a race and she cut across me.
My elbow sprang out, a nudge was all it took.

Now she sits, frog-like,
picking the crusty edge of scab.

I watch and imagine blood-stained tears.

That brother

My bigger and better brother is six foot tall.
His hair is straight as pins and his eyes are a shade of pea.
We're two peas in a pod.

He dresses smart in fancy shirts with swirling paisley patterns.
His denim jeans have rips that show kneecaps bald as skulls.
He's the bee's knees.

He likes to be daring and take up a challenge.
Steals stuff from the market and runs like a flash. Then he got caught.
He's a flash in the pan.

My brother gets moody and quiet at times. Goes under his duvet,
scratches the scars made by blades sharp as thorns.
He's a thorn in my side.

Gagging order

Shame is kindling to silence,
it chokes unspoken words.
My tongue is a slug that fills
the hollow of my mouth.
The first one to talk surrenders
fire to the other.

Twin flight

a dreadful separation
to become individual
facilitates this need
by severing bonds
from she who was
intensely loved:
our Mother

our Mother
intensely loved:
from she who was
by severing bonds
facilitates this need
to become individual
a dreadful separation

Rehearsal

Three hours shy of the alarm, I shuffle words
for a reasoned argument I need to practice.
Lines of talk are left without response.

Your eyes are liquorice, your jaw is set.
I prepare to hear your speech: every word
is testament to the invincible you.

What's a brother?

He's a stain. Sepia spreads in plumes
across table cloths and napkins.

He's a cloud. Head on a periscope
surveying the dips and scrapes of land.

He's a plughole. Gurgling for more,
always needing something to consume.

He's a shopping bag. Crammed with tins,
plus free samples snatched from aisles.

He's a map. Marked with Roman roads,
straight lines that hatch across space.

He's a suit. Fitted at the shoulders,
scarlet lining flashes at the vents.

Like a bead of candle wax he slides,
covering all that went before.

Like a bead of candle wax he slides,
forging a path for me to follow.

Finishing

Stashed on an upper shelf lie the cases. Unzipping them, they slide metal bars and clamping the parts, they test each scooter's strength. The handlebar with daisy stickers belongs to her. He finds balding wheels, evidence of skate park tricks. Jamming brakes bring memories of no-footers and frontslides. In turn, she remembers panther-fast chases. Dragging scooters they find flat tarmac. The rubber grips disintegrate leaving crumbs in a trail. She is not intimidated by his swagger. Reckless he may be but taller now, he has to squat. One foot on the platform, the other scrapes the ground. At the starting line, they count backwards from five, their eyes alive with rivalry. Nudging and barging, they tear at each other's clothes: collide in a heap. Their laughter is a balm upon those earlier years when winning meant the other had to lose.

Starlings

Side-by-side we sit, watching the wipers swipe
pollution-stained raindrops.
You gnaw tags of skin beside your nails,
I grip the steering wheel like a lifebuoy.
Staring ahead, I pose the questions
you don't want to answer.
Talking from the side of your mouth,
you dismiss the concerns that fill my head
like a murmuration of starlings.

Charlotte

He says I must meet her again.
She with the strawberry voice.

He says I will like her now.
She with laughter that ripples.

He says he loves her and needs her.
She with vanilla perfume.

He says she wants to start afresh.
She who is able to slither and melt.

He says she'll drop by to see me again.
She's a chip of dark chocolate, so bitter she stings.

Surprise

Coils in her mother's hair bounce as they chat.
Talk is of clothes that no longer suit.
Is it the cut of her mother's dress,
or the way she stands flat-footed?
Her stomach is a bud
pressing folds of fabric.
A late arrival came five years ago,
the boy a pendant on a string of girls.
Try the five-two diet, the daughter blurts.
The mother smiles: not in her condition.

it got ruined
with one telephone
call. There was no saving
of dates or agreeing of details

accommodations
could not be reached nor
was there an opportunity for
exchanging wishes or greetings

I'll be alone this
Christmas. The first without
family or friends. It all went wrong

on the first
November

Babies

I listen to the two women at the bus stop. Surreptitiously I perch on the bench while they stand firm-footed at the front. The tall one is going into town to buy a matching outfit for herself and her little one. The other responds with enthusiasm and they swap recommendations. How nice. They each have their own little darling, one with the sweetest temperament, the other with the cutest face. I think of babies with downy hair but I've got it all wrong. The tall one says hers has curls tied with a ribbon, the other lets the ebony strands fall in a fringe. Good God – anyone would think this was a competition. But they're not into that sort of thing. It would be a mistake to have sisters compete. I struggle to understand the family dynamics. The women don't look like they're related. One's tall in her tight fitting jeans and the other is dumpy in a raincoat. Who the bloody hell are these people? I'm almost relieved when the number fifty-six arrives and they wait for the doors to open. It's only then I notice the face of a pooch peering from each of their handbags.

Geology of a heart

Serrated cliffs bear scars of bickering and battles:
outcomes from emotional weathering.
From grassy cliff tops, wounds are unobservable,
yet still they undermine and threaten with collapse.

Inland, heaths and moors feed acidic memories:
barren waste from a past that should remain
banished from thought, kept from all consciousness,
yet still low growing shrubs survive and spread.

Motorways dissect like veins and arteries:
carving up the landscape of a heart.
A chance for change hurtles to a future –
the past is left behind without a glance.

Seven stages

Babble of babies in the bathroom
Tantrum of toddlers on the terrace
Scrap of school children in the study
Anger of adolescents in the attic
Presentation of people on the porch
Muddle of middle-aged in the men's
Origami of old-aged in the ossuary

At the care home

You could tell they were sisters
zebra striped mules and leopard print clogs.
Fingers around teacups, their heads at a slant.
Jane's parting was straight, Ellen's fringe in her eyes.

You could tell they were sisters
deep belly cackles and tittering clatter.
Their back teeth showed metal, their lips shaped to ovals,
Jane wore pink lipstick, Ellen's was scarlet.

You could tell they were sisters
thank yous and pleases were never forgotten.
Patience they showed as meals were distributed,
Jane had a napkin, Ellen's went missing.

You could tell they were sisters
You can't leave me, said Ellen. *I can't bear it*, said Jane.
The ambulance came and Jane was transported,
Ellen, left wandering, never saw her again.

Acknowledgements

I am indebted to Sarah Barr and Helen Pizzey for commenting on the manuscript. Thanks to the Wimborne Writing Group for their on-going support and advice. A nod to the Vivo Gang. I give special thanks to the great people at Wordsmith_HQ, especially Dr Sophie-Louise Hyde and Kathryn Cockrill. I'm grateful to Emily Suzanne Young for the fabulous cover design. Also, many thanks to Ian Stephen for writing the foreword.

About Wordsmith_HQ

Wordsmith_HQ is an online, creative platform that supports writers on their writing and publishing journey. With a real focus on life-long learning and professional development related to your writing practice, we help writers to develop their craft and realise their potential.

Through publication and showcasing, online workshops, and key tools and resources, we provide writers with an immersive experience and the interactive support that they need to strengthen their portfolio, build their confidence, and share their writing widely within and beyond our unique Wordsmith community.

Wordsmith_HQ is representative of you—written in honesty and driven by passion—and everyone is welcome.

www.wordsmithhq.co.uk

Also from Wordsmith_HQ

Three Degrees of Separation
by Rachel Lewis

What happens to love when mental illness steps in? Why do some of us get better and some of us stay worse? How do families and friends hold together as the cracks show?

Rachel's debut poetry collection, *Three Degrees of Separation*, explores love, laughter and family survival in the face of mental ill-health across a sequence of poems that will make you smile with sadness and cry with laughter all at once. Her verse is clever and refreshing, beautifully moving yet fun at the same time.